RESPONSIBLE PARENTHOOD
The Politics of Mexico's New Population Policies

Frederick C. Turner

American Enterprise Institute for Public Policy Research
Washington, D. C.

Frederick C. Turner is professor of political science at the
University of Connecticut.

ISBN 0-8447-3140-4

Foreign Affairs Study 13, October 1974

Library of Congress Catalog Card No. 74-18959

Printed in United States of America

CONTENTS

RESPONSIBLE PARENTHOOD

Introduction

In regard to the political difficulties of introducing new policies to limit population increase, Ivan Illich has said, "Only a strongman could afford simultaneously to dare traditional Catholics who speak about sin, communists who want to out-breed the United States imperialists, and nationalists who speak about colonizing vast unsettled expanses." [1]

The President of Mexico, Luis Echeverría Alvarez, has proved to be such a strongman, backed by a powerful and broadly representative party, in a country that has achieved remarkable political stability. During 1972, President Echeverría quietly allowed government agencies to undertake programs that have reversed the official, hands-off policies of the past, so that the national government now educates citizens on family planning and distributes contraceptives to those who require them. In time, these programs may slow Mexico's rate of population growth, which has been one of the highest in the world, and if so, the new orientation should help to offset a series of problems that have been exacerbated by the nation's exceedingly high birthrate.

The new policy raises a number of questions about the nature of Mexican politics and the feasibility of governmental initiatives to deal with the population "explosion." Why did the government decide on the about-face, and how much of a break with the past does it actually represent? How has the government been able to create support for the reorientation in the context of what has been widely assumed to be dedicated opposition from the Catholic Church, the

---

[1] Ivan Illich, "Sexual Power and Political Potency," in David Chaplin, ed., *Population Policies and Growth in Latin America* (Lexington, Mass.: D. C. Heath, 1971), p. 177.

1

nationalists, and the political left? What role has nationalism actually played in this process of change, and what does the process imply for the foreign policy of such countries as the United States? These questions have implications which reach far beyond the borders of Mexico.

1. Mexico's Adaptation to Population Pressure

The degree and the rapidity of adaptation that are evident in Mexico's new population policy are striking indeed. Besides marking a dramatic reversal in the stance of President Echeverría himself, the new position of the government indicates a rejection of a series of arguments that had figured prominently in Mexico during the 1950s and most of the 1960s. Even more significant perhaps, the reorientation stands in contrast to traditional attitudes that survey research had shown to be held by both leaders and ordinary Mexican citizens in recent years. Although the new pronouncements thus signify a major initiative on the part of the executive branch, its efforts in population limitation can gain strength from the very elitism of the Mexican system, from what Arthur Corwin calls "the fact that an elite has always decided for the masses, the fact that the masses are accustomed to government initiative and leadership." [2] As political leaders have become convinced that unbridled population expansion does indeed threaten the social goals of what they define as the "continuing Revolution," their actions in regard to family planning fit appropriately with Mexico's long tradition of governmental activity and concern for the welfare of all citizens.

The most important single shift in the demographic policy of the Mexican government came on January 1, 1973, when the Secretariat of Health and Welfare (*Secretaría de Salubridad y Asistencia*, SSA) began a national program of integral family planning. Commencing initially in the Federal District, Toluca, Cuernavaca, Pachuca, Querétaro, and three other cities, the program is designed to spread throughout the Republic and to include postpartum instruction in family planning in every Mexican hospital.[3] The goal is to cut down significantly on the country's rate of population increase, and in order to do this the medical service of the Mexican Institute of Social Security (*Instituto Mexicano de Seguro Social*) was ordered to begin dispensing

---

[2] Arthur F. Corwin, *Contemporary Mexican Attitudes toward Population, Poverty, and Public Opinion* (Gainesville: University of Florida Press, 1963), p. 50.
[3] Juventino Chávez, "Campaña de salubridad para reducir la natalidad," *Novedades*, January 3, 1973.

2

contraceptives to those who needed assistance in acquiring them. The new policy stresses the need for "responsible parenthood," suggesting that parents must be able to educate and take care of all of the physical and psychological needs of the children whom they bring into the world. The program was announced in conjunction with dramatic news that there are 400,000 recorded abortions in Mexico each year and that there were 2.6 million Mexican births in 1971.[4]

After the program was well under way, its director, Dr. David Fragoso Lizalde, explained that it had two objectives: an educational effort directed toward doctors, nurses, and the general public, and the provision of contraceptives for those who asked for them.[5] The policy has been a major break with the past, and it provides an important opportunity to begin to deal with one of Mexico's most pressing problems.

The government had actually begun a new program in family-planning education before the announcement of this new policy. From late February through early May 1972, an overflow crowd came each Monday evening to a 400-seat auditorium in Mexico City where the National Institute for the Protection of Children (*Instituto Nacional de Protección a la Infancia*, INPI) had arranged the first set of lectures in the country's new School for the Fathers and Mothers of Families (*Escuela para Padres y Madres de Familia*). The series was not limited to fathers and mothers as the name implies, and after its prestigious inauguration by the wife of President Echeverría, its free lectures drew in a wide audience of young and old, men and women, married and unmarried persons. In addition to sessions on the history and techniques of family planning, the series—in a move that was clearly designed to pacify conservatives, nationalists, and militant Catholics —also emphasized the need for family solidarity and discouraged what was called "the introduction of customs and values foreign to the national culture that do not favor the harmonious development of society."[6]

---

[4] *Tiempo*, vol. 61 (May 8, 1972), p. 13. An extensive comparison of the abortion situation in Mexico with that in other countries may be found in Leopoldo Aguilar García, "Política legislativa actual del aborto en México y en el mundo," a paper presented at the XVIII Congreso Nacional de Sociología, Oaxtepec, Morelos, October 20, 1972. While the number of Mexican abortions each year remains highly questionable, governmental announcements on the subject at least demonstrate the concern of the Echeverría administration.

[5] Silvestre González, "El programa de paternidad responsable, a todo el país," *Excelsior*, June 6, 1973.

[6] *Tiempo*, vol. 61 (May 15, 1972), p. 26.

In this enterprise designed to bring more governmental support to the family-planning movement, Dr. Norberto Treviño Zapata, the INPI director, ingeniously made the effort seem to represent a withdrawal rather than an intensification of government influence. With considerable truth, he said, "Neither today nor in the past does any political, governmental system have the humanity needed to sustain the responsibility, reason, judgment, and discernment that the father and mother must personally share." [7] Nevertheless, of course, his words implied that, because of this judgment and discernment, parents might see the need to limit their families. From the INPI series, they could become more aware of the problem, find that the government was concerned to counteract it, and also learn the techniques of family planning.

The limited nature of the program reveals the continuing constraints upon government actions, the feasibility of the new initiatives, and the combination of freedom, paternalism, and rhetoric that fundamentally characterize Mexican politics. In an article entitled "Irresponsible Paternalism," which neatly reverses the government slogan of "responsible parenthood," Abraham López Lara suggests with barbed humor that it is an "ironic dream to hope for responsibility in paternity from a people that for centuries has been paternalistically manipulated in all spheres." How curious, he comments, that liberty and the dignity of the citizen are invoked in regard to family planning when the government rejects them in other areas of policy making.[8] Mexico, with its powerful presidency and interest groups united through the Revolutionary Institutional party (*Partido Revolucionario Institucional*, PRI), has certainly remained paternalistic, although critics of the government (including López Lara) enjoy far more freedom than do Latin Americans living under military authoritarians. The Echeverría initiatives *are* compatible with the norms of individual liberty that have been a lodestar in Mexico since the time of Benito Juárez and the revolutionaries of 1910, but of course, the president has been restrained, not only by his own ideologically shaped view of what is best for the Mexican people, but also by the incipient refusal of public opinion and such influential groups as intellectuals or Catholic leaders, to go along with more stringent measures to limit population growth. The Mexican political system does rely even more upon rhetoric than do most other systems, and the "responsible parenthood" campaign is once again calling forth reiterations about the "Revolution" and the "people," but the program is also respond-

---

[7] Ibid.

[8] Abraham López Lara, "Paternalismo irresponsable," *Excelsior*, June 9, 1973.

4

ing—as far as political constraints will allow—to the needs of the Mexican citizenry.

Mexican periodicals have shown an openness to the new governmental orientation, as can be seen for instance in the favorable letters printed in *Tiempo*. In a typical letter to this influential magazine, Francisco Gálvez Torres distinguished between Mexico's positive program of "family planning" and "responsible parenthood," in which each family decides on the number of children that it can adequately support, and "birth control," which he characterized as leading to thousands of sterilizations in India. In a nationalistic spirit that has also permeated other Mexican responses, Gálvez concluded, "I believe that it is the fundamental duty of all Mexicans to support the programs of family planning." [9] As Martín Luis Guzmán Ferrer said in a signed *Tiempo* editorial, the government action was "a magnificent and highly appropriate initiative that will require, on the part of all Mexicans, a great sensibility, prudence, and feeling of family unity." Guzmán, like other commentators, quite correctly noted that family planning is no panacea for economic underdevelopment, but that, since rapid population increase interferes with savings and lowers the standard of living of Mexican *campesinos* and urban slum dwellers, the government was right to take action against it.[10]

As these positive expressions demonstrate, the government has been wise in not seeking to impose decisions upon individual citizens, but rather to gently attempt to raise the level of consciousness of the population problem and to provide assistance for those who wish to practice family planning. In this, as in other areas of innovation, the Echeverría administration has enjoyed a largely favorable response in the press. It is a sign of the underlying stability of Mexico's political system and the power of the PRI that even such a controversial and traditionally private matter as family planning can be undertaken without violent discord and disruption of the kind that has broken out in regard to student protests since 1968. In the instigation of progressive family-planning programs, the degree of censorship that the government exercises over the press, like its regular co-optation of the Mexican left, may work in the national interest, whatever the deficiencies of censorship and co-optation from other standpoints. As Marvin Alisky has commented in regard to

---

[9] *Tiempo*, vol. 61 (May 29, 1972), p. 4. See also the letters of Dr. Mario B. Aragón, ibid., May 15, 1972; José María Estrada, ibid., April 24, 1972; and Manuel Cabrera, ibid., April 10, 1972. Actually, in 1971 alone, the number of sterilizations in India reached 2.1 million.

[10] Martín Luis Guzmán Ferrer, "Malthus entre nosotros," ibid., May 8, 1972, p. 20.

Marxist opposition to family planning, "There is little evidence that Mexico's child-begetting masses read or hear such arguments, let alone heed them. . . . Marxist support has not been the reason most Mexicans have not purchased contraceptives." [11]

Indeed, spokesmen for the left in Mexico have been far less critical of the government's new orientation than many observers had expected. Octavio Paz, one of the nation's greatest poets, has chided the left for its past actions, saying forcefully that "the adoption of a demographic policy is urgent in Mexico. In this the left has been no less guilty, with its silence, than have been the Government and the Church with their hypocritical complacency." [12] This type of statement, made well before the announcement of the new policies, helped to pave the way for them and to show that men like Paz, who had been so critical of the government's handling of the student disruptions in 1968 and the internal functioning of the PRI, would welcome rather than oppose a shift in policy on population.

After the announcement of the reorientation, a series of articles by Marxist authors in *Siempre!*, one of the most widely read periodicals of the Mexican left, indicated considerable support for Echeverría's stance. Pointing particularly to the difficulties in education, Roberto Blanco Moheno said that Mexico has too many children, referred to the SSA secretary as a "lay saint" for his stress on the responsibility of parents to educate and ethically rear all of their children, and concluded that President Echeverría "has understood the limits of the problem and gotten ready to fight it in the only way in which it can be fought and has to be fought in Mexico: by respecting the liberty of the human person." [13] With full appreciation of the ecological and economic issues involved, Alberto Domingo was most concerned with the human problems that would be brought on by another doubling of the Mexican population in the next twenty years. He noted, quite rightly, that the poorest and weakest members of Mexican society would ultimately be those to suffer most from it.[14] Like many critics on the left, José Luis Ceceña and Antonio Vargas MacDonald blamed the capitalist system rather than the population explosion for the

---

[11] Marvin Alisky, "Mexico versus Malthus: National Trends," *Current History*, vol. 66 (May 1974), p. 202.

[12] Octavio Paz, John Womack, and Frederick C. Turner, "México: Presente y futuro," *Plural*, no. 6 (March 1972), p. 6. This article reproduces a round-table discussion that was held at Harvard University on November 15, 1971.

[13] Roberto Blanco Moheno, "Natalidad y conciencia," *Siempre!*, no. 966 (July 26, 1972), p. 13.

[14] Alberto Domingo, "Natalidad sin freno," *Siempre!*, no. 987 (May 24, 1972), p. 15.

poverty and underemployment of the developing nations, but they nevertheless recognized population growth as aggravating these problems.[15] Vargas typically advocated an end to capitalism and the adoption in Mexico of the kind of socialism that he associated with Mao's China and Fidel Castro's Cuba, but he said that "if the policy of our government does not aim at a radical transformation of the economic system, but only institutes limited reforms, then it must necessarily adopt a position on the explosive growth of population, that is, a demographic policy" like that announced by the SSA.[16]

The reactions of Mexican Marxists have thus been flexible rather than dogmatic. The fundamental Marxist interpretation, which finds systematic exploitation rather than population growth to be the major cause of poverty and want, naturally emphasizes social reorganization rather than contraception as the required direction for social policy. Although some Marxists have gone so far as to oppose family planning because it removes one source of the pressure that is so necessary to bring about a complete reorientation of economic relationships, spokesmen for the left in Mexico have generally supported President Echeverría's policies on the pragmatic grounds that family planning can improve the situation of Mexico's poor and that the president is also taking other measures to redistribute income and to open the PRI to a broader range of opinion. Even the leaders of the left-wing, but regularly co-opted, Popular Socialist party (Partido Popular Socialista, PPS) have chosen to denounce the United States rather than the initiatives of Echeverría. In the Chamber of Deputies debates over the new population law, which incorporates the Echeverría policies, PPS Deputy Pánfilo Orozco decried the idea "of North American imperialism's control of birth in the underdeveloped countries, its sterilization of men and women." [17] Despite such rhetoric, when the law came to a vote, it passed unanimously.

The limits of the new policy provide another reason for its acceptance. Even if former President Nixon's science adviser, Dr. Lee DuBridge, is right in saying that "every human institution—school, university, church, family, government and international agency"— should establish as a prime task the achievement of zero population

---

[15] José Luis Ceceña, "En todo caso, la planeación familiar no es la respuesta," Siempre!, no. 985 (May 10, 1972), pp. 20-21.

[16] Antonio Vargas MacDonald, "Ser mexicano es ser macho, ser macho es tener muchos hijos; Muertos de hambre? Allá Dios y ellos párenle!" Siempre!, no. 986 (May 17, 1972), pp. 22-23.

[17] Angel T. Ferreira, "Tras de 30 discursos se aprobó la Ley de Población," Excelsior, November 28, 1973.

growth,[18] most of the families and the leaders of the Church, the government, and the universities in Mexico do not yet agree with him. It would be unrealistic to expect them to work in Mexico—any more than they do in the United States—toward the goal of zero population. Nevertheless, some of Mexico's prominent intellectuals do already advocate advanced positions and show deep understanding of the relationship between changing attitudes on family planning and the evolution of social roles and marital relationships. For example, Luis Leñero Otero writes that "without doubt, contraception represents, in many cases, an efficient and necessary means of feminine defense and liberation from the man when he does not participate in conjugal life with a sense of unity, equality and respect for his wife."[19] Although government officials do not speak of "liberation," it is clear that the presidential position has shifted greatly. In this regard, when the wife of President Echeverría was questioned about her views on the population explosion, she advocated conscientious parenthood, noted her work through the INPI to spread family education, and said that "if in my day there had been talk of family planning, I would have taught courses in it."[20] This is a strong endorsement from the mother of eight children and the wife of a man who had, in his recent electoral campaign and afterwards, rejected family planning and praised the large size of Mexico's population.

The sharp break with the past stands out even more clearly when the new orientation is compared to older Mexican doctrines on population. Before Luis Echeverría took office on December 1, 1970, the basic position of his predecessor, President Gustavo Díaz Ordaz, had been that, although rapid population growth might aggravate some of Mexico's problems, the country's greatest asset was its human potential, and economic development would have to be based on the realization of that potential. The assumption was that "the exceptional rate of population expansion requires far more rapid economic growth."[21] Such sentiments were widespread among Mexi-

---

[18] Quoted by William H. Draper, Jr., in "Is Zero Population Growth the Answer?" a speech delivered at the Shoreham Hotel, Washington, D. C., December 2, 1969.

[19] Luis Leñero Otero, "The Mexican Urbanization Process and Its Implications," *Demography*, vol. 5 (1968), p. 870.

[20] From an interview of María Esther Zuno de Echeverría by Luis Suárez, *Siempre!*, no. 987 (May 24, 1972), pp. 32-33.

[21] Roberto Amorós, ed., *Ideas políticas del Presidente Gustavo Díaz Ordaz* (México: Editorial Ruta, 1966), pp. 87-89. On the staunch opposition of Echeverría himself to family planning before 1972, see Terry L. McCoy, "A Paradigmatic Analysis of Mexican Population Policy," in McCoy, ed., *The Dynamics of Population Policy in Latin America* (Cambridge, Mass.: Ballinger Publishing Company, 1974), pp. 396-397.

can elites during the 1960s, when they saw the economic advance of their nation as being such that there did not appear to be an immediate need for family planning in order to keep per capita gross national product moving consistently ahead. A sample of leadership opinion revealed that some 72 percent of those interviewed saw the country developing quickly, while only 5 percent perceived serious problems of a collective nature. Half of the respondents looked upon Mexico's heavy population increase as leading to economic power, and only 13 percent believed that a time of economic impoverishment was approaching. While 40 percent of the leaders considered the population explosion to have grave dimensions, 55 percent saw it as unimportant. As the director of the survey commented, it tended to show that the leaders were "more conformists than revolutionaries." [22]

The statements of Mexican demographers, made in the 1950s and 1960s before the impact of demographic change had become so apparent, usually reflected the same sentiments. Given the fact that Mexico's population reached 50 million late in 1970, and the fact that its population increase in the coming decade should at least equal the total number of citizens in the Republic when the 1910 Revolution broke out (15 million), it now seems almost anachronistic to look back on older demographic volumes like that of Julio Durán Ochoa, who set Mexico's population at 29 million when his comprehensive treatise was published in 1955. In the traditional vein, he called for more effective industrialization to absorb migrants from the agricultural sector, for the better protection and utilization of natural resources, and for more rational internal redistributions of Mexico's population, without once calling for a parallel program that would assist Mexican families to have only the number of children that they actually desire.[23]

Similarly, in 1962, Gilberto Loyo declared that the population explosion had both negative and stimulating effects on the national economy, and that Mexicans should deal with their social problems by furthering economic development rather than by limiting population growth.[24] He went so far as to add that "Mexico can, for the rest of

---

[22] Luis Leñero Otero, *Investigación de la familia en México: Presentación y avance de resultados de una encuesta nacional* (México: Instituto Mexicano de Estudios Sociales, 1968), pp. 179-180.

[23] Julio Durán Ochoa, *Población* (México: Fondo de Cultura Económica, 1955), pp. 266-267.

[24] See "Notas sobre población y desarrollo económico," the second of three sections in Gilberto Loyo, *Población y desarrollo económico* (México: Selección de

this century, concentrate on economic development without worrying about a policy to restrict births, which would neither be justified nor have the results hoped for by its authors and executors."[25] Even Raúl Benítez Zenteno, who was to become the director of the *Mexican Review of Sociology (Revista Mexicana de Sociología)*, contended that "direct action" to limit population was not necessary, because, with increases in urbanization, education, and the standard of living, Mexico's fertility rate would automatically drop.[26] Although Benítez favored the wider dissemination of sex education and contraceptive devices so that those parents wishing to limit the size of their families could do so more easily and more safely,[27] he still argued that economic underdevelopment caused high population increase rather than vice versa, that "in no way can it be established that conditions of backwardness arise from a high level of demographic growth."[28]

The attitudes of demographers and the political elite coincided with ignorance or rejection of new contraceptive practices on the part of most Mexicans. In a national sampling conducted in Mexico during 1966, only 31.1 percent of the respondents said that they used contraceptive techniques. Of these, 63 percent used the rhythm method, and 16 percent used the pill.[29] Earlier data reveal that women in Mexico City used birth control measures far less than did women in such other Latin American cities as San José, Panama City, Caracas, and Rio de Janeiro.[30] Cultural norms encourage large families in rural Mexico as well as in the urban centers. In such communities as San Bernardino Contla, for example, young men feel considerable pressure

---

Estudios Latinoamericanos, 1963), esp. pp. 155-156, 179-182, 190-191. This section was first presented to the Sociedad Mexicana de Planificación in August 1962.

[25] Gilberto Loyo, *La población de México, estado actual y tendencias, 1960-1980* (México: Editorial Cultura, 1960), pp. 133-135, 137.

[26] Raúl Benítez Zenteno, *Análisis demográfico de México* (México: Instituto de Investigaciones Sociales, Universidad Nacional Autónoma de México, 1961), pp. 81, 97-99.

[27] Ibid., p. 86. Also, see Loyo, *Población y desarrollo económico*, pp. 171-172.

[28] Raúl Benítez Zenteno, "Cambios demográficos y la población en México," *Revista Mexicana de Sociología*, vol. 30 (July-September 1968), p. 689.

[29] Oscar Maldonado, *Los católicos y la planeación familiar: Resultados de una encuesta nacional* (México: Instituto Mexicano de Estudios Sociales, 1969), pp. 122, 133. Some 68.9 percent of the respondents did not practice contraception; 38.9 percent said that they were ignorant concerning it; and 30 percent said that they understood it but did not use it.

[30] J. Mayone Stycos, *Human Fertility in Latin America: Sociological Perspectives* (Ithaca: Cornell University Press, 1968), p. 299.

to marry and raise children, since they are excluded from the religious and ceremonial life of the community until they do so.[31]

This desire for large families underlies the traditional rejection of contraception. At least in the case of Mexico, Paul Schultz is correct in saying that "fundamentally, the problem is social; parents want more children than are needed to replace themselves." [32] When asked in 1966 how many children made up an ideal family, only 17.7 percent of the men and women in a Mexican national sample replied that fewer than four children did, while 23.8 percent said that more than six children were ideal.[33] Mexicans want larger families than do the citizens of nearly all other nations, both inside and outside Latin America. As Table 1 indicates, the "ideal" number of children among urban Mexicans has been far higher than among urbanites in Colombia, Venezuela, Brazil, and other nations. Whereas urban Mexicans give 4.2 as the ideal number of children, a national sample including rural residents produced the higher figure of 5.3 children, which, as Table 2 suggests, is far larger than that for many other national samples in the 1960s.

The Mexican desire for many children is not immutable. Attitudes toward population planning can change very rapidly in some

Table 1

"IDEAL" NUMBER OF CHILDREN DESIRED BY URBAN RESIDENTS OF SEVERAL COUNTRIES

Country	Ideal Number of Children
Mexico	4.2
Colombia	3.8
Costa Rica	3.6
Panama	3.5
Venezuela	3.5
Brazil	2.7

Source: Adapted from data in Reuben Hill, "Research on Human Fertility," *International Social Science Journal*, vol. 20 (1968), p. 233.

[31] Hugo G. Nutini, *San Bernardino Contla: Marriage and Family Structure in a Tlaxcalan Municipio* (Pittsburgh: University of Pittsburgh Press, 1968), p. 250.

[32] T. Paul Schultz, "The Economics of Population Policy: A Neglected Field of Priority Research," in *Mankind's Great Need: Population Research* (Washington, D. C.: Population Crisis Committee, 1971), p. 56.

[33] Maldonado, *Los católicos y la planeación familiar*, p. 118.

Table 2

"IDEAL" NUMBER OF CHILDREN DESIRED BY CITIZENS OF SEVERAL COUNTRIES IN NATIONAL SAMPLES

Country	Ideal Number of Children
Mexico	5.3
Philippines	5.0
Turkey	3.5
United States	3.3
Puerto Rico	3.0
Japan	2.8
France	2.7
Hungary	2.4

Source: Adapted from data in Luis Leñero Otero, *Investigación de la familia en México: Presentación y avance de resultados de una encuesta nacional* (México: Instituto Mexicano de Estudios Sociales, 1968), pp. 179-180; and Reuben Hill, "Research on Human Fertility," *International Social Science Journal*, vol. 20 (1968), p. 233.

contexts, as in the United States, where the proportion of persons believing that the decision on having an abortion should be left up to women and their doctors rose from about 15 percent in 1968 to 64 percent in 1972. Some 56 percent of the Catholics in the United States had come to agree with this liberal position on abortion, while 68 percent of the Catholics said that birth control services should be provided for unmarried teenagers.[34] Survey research reveals that the better-educated respondents are far more liberal in regard to these issues than are those with fewer years of formal schooling, and since the proportion of residents at higher education levels is far lower in Mexico than in the United States—as well as because of the quite different cultural contexts of the two countries—it remains doubtful that beliefs in Mexico will change with anything like the rapidity with which they have shifted north of the Rio Bravo. Nevertheless, especially with the Mexican government coming to place its prestige and influence behind responsible family planning, Mexican attitudes should become considerably more liberal as time goes on.

[34] *New York Times*, August 25, 1972.

2. Forces behind the New Orientation

Since the 1972 initiatives in family planning mark an abrupt, far-reaching change from the past policies of the Mexican government, it is important to analyze why they came about. One evident cause was the precipitate downturn in Mexico's rate of economic growth in 1971, which made the liabilities of the population explosion stand out at a time when the Echeverría administration was working cautiously to rectify extreme inequalities in income distribution and the standard of living among the different social classes and regions of the Republic. Of more long-term significance were new demographic studies and a shifting intellectual climate, as well as the fact that the extent of population growth during the 1960s proved to be far more rapid than had been predicted at the beginning of the decade. Less influence derived from the frequently mentioned factors of the nation's exceedingly high rate of illegal abortions and the increased questioning of traditional positions within the Catholic Church, because, although these elements may have had some impact on the governmental reorientation, neither the abortion situation nor the stance of the Church had changed enough to bring on a sudden alteration in government policy. Political pressure has been a primary reason why Latin American governments have not undertaken more forceful policies of population control,[35] and political considerations ultimately lie behind the modification of governmental positions as well. But it must be recognized that these pressures and considerations themselves have arisen out of the economic, cultural, and religious contexts of Latin American societies.

As was noted above, a falling off in the pace of economic growth during 1971 was a principal cause for the demographic reorientation by the Echeverría administration. Shortly before the announcement of the new population policy, it was predicted that the government would not change its position until an economic decline became evident,[36] and this prediction appears to have been accurate: the poor performance of the Mexican economy during 1971 influenced the new policies of 1972. According to some estimates, the yearly advance of the gross national product fell from over 6 percent to only 3.1 percent in 1971, while the annual rate of population increase went from

[35] On this point, see Gustavo Pérez Ramírez, "Family Planning and Research in Latin America, 1965," in *The Problem of Population: Educational Considerations* (Notre Dame: University of Notre Dame Press, 1965), p. 166.

[36] Paz, Womack, and Turner, "México: Presente y futuro," p. 6.

13

3.5 percent to 4.41 percent.[37] A more conservative, business-oriented source placed the population rise at 3.4 percent and that of the GNP at 4 percent in 1971, but this still meant that the increase in real per capita product reached only 0.4 percent in 1971.[38] Such a negative turn in the rate of development, where population growth equals or surpasses economic gains, has been common in a number of other countries, but it has remained so far from Mexico's experience that even the spectre of it for a single year is enough to produce significant shifts in policy.

Investments in population planning can yield very impressive results in terms of per capita product and savings on future educational costs,[39] and in an economy that has undergone a sharp decline, these advantages come to take on particular appeal. Although 1972 brought significant economic recovery and an upsurge in investment, the fundamental problem of low purchasing power for the great majority of Mexicans continued to emphasize the need for maintaining or expanding the new stance on population growth. It is only logical that, as Mexico's powerful minister of government (*Gobernación*), Mario Moya Palencia, told an enthusiastic congregation of legislators and onlookers in the Chamber of Deputies late in 1973, "the solution" to many Mexican problems is to increase the size of the economic pie while reducing the number of mouths needing to eat from it.[40]

When one looks for historical parallels to the recent circumstances of Mexico, it is revealing to see that a drop in per capita income also preceded the administration of Lázaro Cárdenas, which did so much to change the pattern of Mexican politics. If gross domestic product is analyzed in five-year periods since the subsiding of the violence of the 1910 Revolution, the only period in which it fell in per capita terms was in 1930-1934. Whereas every other five-year period since 1925 showed at least a minimum yearly increase

---

[37] José Alvarado, "Menos panes y más bocas: Nuestro desarrollo baja a nivel mínimo," *Siempre!*, no. 985 (May 10, 1972), p. 10.

[38] Marynka Olizar, *A Guide to the Mexican Markets*, 5th ed. (México: n.p., 1972), p. 261. Also, see "Mexico: Ways Through the Economic Thicket," *Latin America*, vol. 6 (February 25, 1972).

[39] Two useful studies on these savings are Leonard G. Bower, "The Return from Investment in Population Control in Less Developed Countries," *Demography*, vol. 5 (1968); and Eduardo E. Arriaga, "Impact of Population Changes on Education Cost," ibid., vol. 9 (May 1972). See also Tomas Frejka, *The Future of Population Growth: Alternative Paths to Equilibrium* (New York: John Wiley & Sons, 1973).

[40] Many statements from this four-hour speech appear in "Revolución demográfica, preconiza Moya," an article by Angel Trinidad Ferreira in *Excelsior*, October 17, 1973.

of 2.2 percent in this figure, it declined by 2.1 percent a year between 1930 and 1934,[41] suggesting one reason why Cárdenas worked to fundamentally reform Mexican politics during the next six years. His restructuring of the Revolutionary party, his distributions of land to *campesinos*, his lessening and counterbalancing of the political power of the Mexican military, his nationalization of foreign oil companies, and his outstanding example of a national leader primarily concerned with the welfare of the common people, all worked to revive and enliven the reformist ethos of the Revolution.

President Echeverría has undertaken dialogue with the left, a firm stance in regard to foreign investment, and somewhat more populist policies than his predecessor on taxation, housing, and the minimum wage. This orientation, which began before the disappointing economic results of Echeverría's first year in office, is clearly reminiscent of Lázaro Cárdenas. Echeverría's subsequent, dramatic demographic reforms showed similar concern for the common people, but the latter reforms may also in part be reactions against a serious downturn in per capita growth, a downturn intriguingly similar to that which originally confronted Cárdenas and encouraged policies that were as strikingly new in the 1930s as is Echeverría's demographic reorientation in the 1970s.

When the economic problems of 1971 are viewed in the context of other statistics, it is even easier to see why family planning became so important. Table 3 contrasts information on demographic and economic development for thirteen Western Hemisphere nations. As is evident, Mexican economic growth per capita had been substantial during the years immediately before 1971, despite the country's exceptionally rapid rate of population increase. Notwithstanding pockets of grave poverty and highly unequal income distribution, Mexico's aggregate level of income per capita had risen far beyond that of such countries as Brazil or Peru. Although not particularly great in comparison to Guatemala, Mexican population density is high in relation both to its amount of arable land and to the densities of the other major nations of the Americas. Its population was doubling every twenty-one years, as compared to fifty-eight years for Argentina. Projections called for 135 million Mexicans in the year 2000, so that given a population of only 15 million in 1910, Mexico's great Revolution for "land and liberty" had broken out at a time when the pressure of population was nine times less than that projected for the end of the century.

---

[41] See Cuadro VIII-1 in *Dinámica de la población de México* (México: Centro de Estudios Económicos y Demográficos, El Colegio de México, 1970).

Table 3

POPULATION AND ECONOMIC GROWTH RATES IN SELECTED COUNTRIES OF NORTH, CENTRAL, AND SOUTH AMERICA

	1972 Rate of Population Increase [a] (percent)	Rate of Population Increase, 1963–1972 [b] (percent)	1972 Density of Population [b] (in persons per sq. kil.)	Yearly Rate of Economic Growth Per Capita, 1965–1970 [c]	National Income Per Capita, 1970 [c] (in U.S. $)	Estimated Population in Year 2000 [a] (in millions)
Mexico	3.4	3.5	27	3.4%	632	135.0
Ecuador	3.4	3.4	23	—	250	16.1
Honduras	3.3	3.1	24	(2.7) [f]	264	7.2
Colombia	3.2	3.2	20	2.4	366	56.7
Venezuela	3.1	3.4	12	0.4	854	26.1
Peru	3.1	3.1	11	—	363	33.4
Panama	3.0	3.0	20	4.5	646	3.6
Brazil	2.8	2.9	12	(3.6) [f]	379	215.5
Guatemala	2.7	2.9	50	2.6	337	12.3
Chile	1.8	(2.3) [d]	(11.3) [e]	1.1	678	16.1
Argentina	1.3	1.5	9	2.6	978	35.3
Uruguay	1.2	1.2	17	0.4	773	4.0
U.S.A.	0.8	1.1	22	2.3	4,294	275.3 [g]

a With the exception of the United States, all data are from *Population and Family Planning in Latin America*, Report No. 17 of the Victor-Bostrom Fund (Fall 1973). United States data are from the *Statistical Abstract of the United States, 1973*, 94th annual edition (Washington, D.C.: United States Department of Commerce, 1973).

b With the exception of Chile, all data are from the *Demographic Yearbook, 1972* (New York: United Nations, 1973). Since this source did not provide information for Chile, the Chilean statistics were taken from Charles Lewis Taylor and Michael C. Hudson, *World Handbook of Political and Social Indicators*, 2nd ed. (New Haven, Conn.: Yale University Press, 1972).

c Source: *Statistical Yearbook, 1972* (New York: United Nations, 1973).

d For the years 1950–1965.

e For 1964.

f The figures for Honduras and Brazil are for the period from 1965 to 1969, while all others in the column are for 1965 to 1970.

g The *Statistical Abstract of the United States* provides three projections for the United States population in the year 2000. Since these range from 250.6 million to 300.4 million, a middle-range figure of 275.3 was entered above.

In the 1970s, Mexican policy makers certainly have attributed major significance to the impact and interrelationship of demographic and economic statistics. This was most evident in data revealed in April 1972 by Mexico's secretary of health and welfare, Dr. Jorge Jiménez Cantú. Not only did the death rate decrease from 33.3 to 9.9 per thousand during the sixty years after 1910, but the absolute number of deaths actually fell from 505,000 in 1910, when Mexico had a total population of 15 million, to 485,600 deaths in 1970, when the total population had risen to about 50 million. As the secretary was careful to point out at the same time, 38 percent of the population still did not drink milk, 23 percent did not eat eggs, and 20 percent went without meat, while housing remained very overcrowded and 38 percent of Mexico's homes lacked potable water.[42] Carrying forward this line of reasoning, a former Mexican undersecretary of health declared at the Third Congress of Mexico's National Academy of Medicine in 1974 that, partially as a result of population pressures, nearly two-thirds of the country's population is endemically undernourished, as "dwarfish" mothers bear malnourished children, deprive them of sustenance in order to feed the later children that come along, and watch them grow up apathetic, mentally slow, and unable to contribute to social progress.[43]

Of particular concern to government officials has been the effect of population growth on employment opportunities. Antonio Carrillo Flores, a leading Mexican intellectual and statesman, argues that governments throughout Latin America came in the late 1960s to be more concerned with population growth "because a stage had been reached in which the number of persons attaining working age every year was increasing rapidly: the problems of urban marginality, structural unemployment and underutilization of human resources were becoming increasingly urgent."[44] Other government officials estimate that 14 million new jobs must be created in Mexico during the next decade, requiring a level of investment that seems to be so high that the public and private sectors cannot meet it.[45]

To gain in efficiency and international competitiveness, Mexican industry has increasingly turned to automation and to investments

---

[42] See "Salud y otros temas," *Tiempo*, vol. 60 (April 10, 1972).

[43] *Excelsior*, January 25, 1974.

[44] Antonio Carrillo Flores, "The Significance of the World Population Conference," *Population and Family Planning in Latin America*, Report No. 17 of the Victor-Bostrom Fund (Fall 1973), p. 11. See also "En la transición demográfica," *Tiempo*, vol. 63 (December 31, 1973), pp. 14-16; and *Novedades*, August 8, 1972.

[45] "Mexico: Export or Bust," *Latin America*, vol. 6 (August 4, 1972), p. 245.

are capital-intensive rather than labor-intensive, but these meas-
have reduced employment in such industries as cotton textiles.[46]
nerous studies have stressed the problems of underemployment
low productivity in many areas of Mexican agriculture.[47] Esti-
es in the Mexican press during 1974 pointed to 2 million Mexicans,
ome 15 percent of the work force, as unemployed, going on to
gest that the unemployment rate would double to 30 percent in
ıy Third World countries by the year 2000.[48] Many critics believe
official unemployment figure of 15 percent to be too low, with
most pessimistic estimates running as high as 40 percent.[49] Since
rent additions to the labor force depend upon the level of fertility
een or twenty years ago, the Mexican government cannot reduce
temporary employment pressures with family-planning measures,
at least such measures can help to prevent the employment
ıation from becoming even more acute in times to come.

The combination of accelerated population increase and faltering
nomic growth seemed even more dangerous to the Echeverría
ninistration because, in 1971, it had moved to assuage criticism
ough modest redistributions of income. During the 1960s, income
tribution was far more skewed in Mexico than in the United States
ν. the United Kingdom, and somewhat more skewed than in such
Latin American countries as Argentina, Brazil, and Colombia.[50] The
data on income levels compiled by Ifigenia de Navarrete, a respected
Mexican economist, suggest a need for redistribution, as do her

---

[46] For useful estimates of the effects of automation on the high costs of
capitalizing new jobs in Mexico, see Melvin L. DeFleur, William V. D'Antonio,
and Lois B. DeFleur, Sociology: Man in Society (Glenview, Ill.: Scott, Foresman,
1971), p. 256.

[47] Among the statements of this position, see Daniel Moreno, Los factores
demográficos en la planeación económica (México: Ediciones de la Cámara
Nacional de la Industria de la Transformación, 1958), pp. 57-62; Harold L.
Geisert, Population Problems in Mexico and Central America (Washington, D. C.:
Population Research Project, George Washington University, 1959), p. 28; Ifigenia
M. de Navarrete, Sobrepoblación y desarrollo económico (México: Universidad
Nacional Autónoma de México, 1967), pp. 20-27; David Ibarra, Ifigenia M. de
Navarrete, Leopoldo Solis, and Víctor L. Urquidi, El perfil de México en 1980
(México: Siglo Veintiuno Editores, 1970), pp. 126-131; México: La política
económica del nuevo gobierno (México: Banco Nacional de Comercio Exterior,
1971), pp. 74-75; and Confrontación sobre problemas económicas, Palacio Na-
cional, 17 de mayo, 1971 (Cuadernos de Documentación, Serie Documentos, No. 1;
México: Secretaría de la Presidencia, 1971), pp. 21-22, 27-29.

[48] Excelsior, February 2, 1974.

[49] James Nelson Goodsell, "Is Their Future Mortgaged by 'Too Many Mexicans'?"
Christian Science Monitor, July 31, 1973.

[50] "Income Distribution in Latin America," Economic Bulletin for Latin America,
vol. 12 (October 1967).

eloquent pleas for the democratization and increased egalitarianism that would accompany such a policy.[51] As Luis Echeverría's attempts to help the lower classes have seemed to threaten a continuation of rapid economic growth, the concern for redistribution has found a natural corollary in the limitation of population increase.

Since reduction in the rate of population growth is generally conceded to spur economic development,[52] it is logical that Mexican officials would want to limit population increments when—on other grounds—they had undertaken policies that cut into the fast-burgeoning gross national product. Echeverría's inaugural address claimed that an "inevitable dilemma" might not exist between redistribution and rapid economic development, but his first year in office proved that economic growth was much slower after the introduction of mildly redistributive policies than it had been before them. Further moves toward wider income distribution were likely once again to increase consumption but to reduce the amount of capital available for reinvestment. At least some evidence of redistribution was necessary, however, in order to maintain the ethical validity of the Mexican Revolution. The real wages of workers and peasants had borne the brunt of industrialization costs between 1940 and 1970, leaving a more and more wealthy elite to live in a style of luxury and expensive display reminiscent of the Porfirian aristocrats against whom the Revolution of 1910 had erupted. Nationalistic protestations continued to refer to the equality of all Mexicans, yet, until President Echeverría imposed a 10 percent luxury tax in 1971, governmental rhetoric on egalitarianism was coming to be less and less believable. The state-

---

[51] Ifigenia M. de Navarrete, "La distribución del ingreso en México: Tendencias y perspectivas," in Ibarra and others, *El perfil de México en 1980*. Her more recent findings are reported in *Excelsior*, November 4, 1973. She finds, for instance, that in 1963 the bottom 10 percent of Mexican families accounted for only 1.9 percent of the national income, while the top 10 percent of the families enjoyed 49.9 percent of the income. Compare "La distribución del ingreso," ch. 7 in Leopoldo Solís, *La realidad económica mexicana: Retrovisión y perspectivas* (México: Siglo Veintiuno Editores, 1970); Jesús Prieto Vásquez, "La distribución del ingreso en México," in Cutberto Díaz Gómez, ed., *México: Sus necesidades, sus recursos* (México: Editora Técnica, 1970); and Morris Singer, *Growth, Equality, and the Mexican Experience* (Austin: University of Texas Press, 1969).

[52] Among the most succinct and convincing summaries of the arguments in this regard are Rubens Vas da Costa, "Crecimiento de la población y desarrollo económico," *Demografía y Economía*, vol. 4 (1970); and Frank W. Notestein, "Some Economic Aspects of Population Change in the Developing Countries," in J. Mayone Stycos and Jorge Arias, eds., *Population Dilemma in Latin America* (Washington, D. C.: Potomac Books, 1966). See also Ansley J. Coale and Edgar M. Hoover, *Population Growth and Economic Development in Low-Income Countries* (Princeton: Princeton University Press, 1958).

ments of political leaders now emphasize the importance of real achievement as opposed to talk about achievement.[53] It was partly the country's economic reorientation toward the needs of the poor [54] (which was required to maintain ideological credibility) that also suggested the significance of initiatives in family planning, to which some of the most outspoken nationalists had traditionally objected.

Another factor underlying the new population policy in Mexico has been past underestimation of the rate of growth. Because a number of projections of Mexican population growth done in the 1950s and early 1960s have proved to be far too low, it is natural for government officials to be wary of such judgments in planning for the future. Just as 1960 census data startled many observers in regard to the absence of fertility declines in various Latin American countries,[55] later data have contained disconcerting surprises for Mexican planners. Louis Ducoff most gravely miscalculated the rapidity of Mexico's growth before the 1960 data were at hand. Whereas the population reached about 50 million late in 1970, he provided three estimates for that year: a low assumption of 38.9 million, a medium assumption of 41.7 million, and a high assumption of 44.9 million. Mexico has already passed Ducoff's low and medium projections for 1980, and even if the country enters into a vigorous national program of family planning during the last part of the 1970s, it is sure to surpass his high projection of 61.7 million.[56]

Ducoff's projections were analyzed and widely discussed in Mexico by demographer Gilberto Loyo and others, although Loyo himself suggested that it would be best to plan on the somewhat higher assumptions of a population of 54.5 million in 1975 and

[53] See, for example, Francisco Cárdenas Cruz, "El país demanda revolución de hechos, advierte Baz al PRI: La paciencia popular, limitada," *Excelsior*, June 29, 1972.

[54] On the early dimensions of this program, see *México: La política económica del nuevo gobierno*, ch. 3, "Crecimiento económico con redistribución del ingreso." Further discussions include "Why Mexico Is in Trouble," *U.S. News & World Report*, April 8, 1974; and Frederick C. Turner, "Mexican Politics: The Direction of Development," in William P. Glade and Stanley R. Ross, eds., *Críticas constructivas del sistema político mexicano* (Austin, Tex.: Institute of Latin American Studies, University of Texas at Austin, 1973).

[55] Eduardo Arriaga goes so far as to say that "not until the 1960's censuses revealed that Latin America was experiencing an unprecedented population growth did a general concern about the extremely high fertility arise." Eduardo E. Arriaga, "The Nature and Effects of Latin America's Non-Western Trend in Fertility," *Demography*, vol. 7 (November 1970), p. 497.

[56] Louis J. Ducoff, *Human Resources of Central America, Panama, and Mexico, 1950-1980, in Relation to Some Aspects of Economic Development* (New York: United Nations, Economic Commission for Latin America, 1960), p. 121.

64.4 million in 1980.[57] Other Mexican estimates similarly gauged the population increase to be lower than it would actually become,[58] while more recent and reasonable, if frightening, projections point to a Mexican population of 71 million in 1980, 99 million in 1990, and 135 million in the year 2000.[59]

Furthermore, the rate of growth in Mexico's national *rate* of population increase has risen significantly in each decade since the Revolution. Counteracting the assumptions of the theory of the demographic transition—the notion that urbanization would lead to an inevitable decline in fertility—on which many demographers had based their optimism, studies in the late-1960s found fertility to have been increasing in urban areas of Mexico. This apparently occurred because of an influx of high-fertility migrants from rural areas and because improved standards of living had encouraged more births from traditionalistic, nonliterate parents who could "afford" more children and saw no reason not to have them.[60] By 1973, with about a fifth of the Mexican population living in greater Mexico City, the capital threatened to become the largest city in the Western Hemisphere by 1980, despite government plans to impede its growth. Almost half of the population was under the age of seventeen, with some estimates suggesting that this proportion would be under fifteen years of age in 1980.[61] This phenomenon emphasizes that fertility

---

[57] "Población de México: Estado actual y tendencias, 1960-1980," in Loyo, *Población y desarrollo económico*, pp. 42-48. This work, which was originally presented in November 1959 to the Instituto Mexicano de Recursos Naturales No Renovables, was also published as a separate book.

[58] Raúl Benítez Zenteno correctly estimated that Mexico's population would reach 49.2 million in 1970, although he seems to have been too low in his projection of 61.9 million in 1980. Benítez Zenteno, *Análisis demográfico de México*, pp. 108-109. See also Raúl Benítez Zenteno and Gustavo Cabrera Acevedo, *Proyecciones de la población de México, 1960-1980* (México: Banco de México, 1966); Philippe Bourcier de Carbon, "Précision sur les perspectives de population active. Application au Mexique," *Population*, vol. 25 (January-February 1970); and Ricardo Alvarado, "México: Proyecciones de la población total (1960-2000) y de la población economicamente activa (1960-1985)," *Revista Mexicana de Sociología*, vol. 32 (September-October 1970).

[59] *Dinámica de la población de México*, p. 192.

[60] Alvan O. Zarate, "Fertility in Urban Areas of Mexico: Implications for the Theory of the Demographic Transition," *Demography*, vol. 4 (1967), pp. 372-373; Zarate, "Differential Fertility in Monterrey, Mexico: Prelude to Transition?" *Milbank Memorial Fund Quarterly*, vol. 45 (April 1967), part 1, p. 105; and Zarate, "Some Factors Associated with Urban-Rural Fertility Differentials," *Population Studies*, vol. 21 (November 1967), pp. 288, 292.

[61] Goodsell, "Is Their Future Mortgaged by 'Too Many Mexicans'?" For more detailed demographic statistics, see the latest edition of the *Anuario estadístico de los Estados Unidos Mexicanos*, published by the Secretaría de Industria y Comercio, Dirección General de Estadística.

depends on popular mores and that urbanization by itself will not automatically curb the population explosion. As a result of these findings and the contrast between Mexico's demographic experience and the predictions made about it, population planning now seems quite rational.

By the time of the shift in government policy in 1972, the climate of intellectual opinion had also changed greatly from what it had been only ten years earlier. During the middle 1960s, foreign observers began to stress that a one-third decrease in Mexico's birth rate would lead to "an enormous betterment in human welfare," [62] and by the end of the decade even Gilberto Loyo had modified the categorical nature of his earlier stand.[63] During this period, social scientists related overpopulation to Mexico's *jacales*, the squatter settlements built with discarded materials,[64] and found that fast-paced urbanization, when combined with the maintenance of high birth rates and lengthening life spans, had caused severe shortages of schools and water facilities.[65] Some observers even felt that it threatened to downgrade and radicalize the public universities,[66] while survey research indicated that over half of the Mexican women studied felt that marriage and their child-bearing responsibilities had interfered with the realization of their own personal capabilities.[67] In 1970, a study done at the Center for Economic and Demographic Studies (*Centro de Estudios Económicos y Demográficos*) warned that precipitant population

---

[62] Joseph A. Kahl and J. Mayone Stycos, "Filosofía de la política demográfica en Latinoamérica," *El Trimestre Económico*, vol. 30 (July-September 1964), p. 432. This article was later republished in *Estudios de Población y Desarrollo*, vol. 1 (1967).

[63] He wrote: "This strong Mexican demographic growth is not, by itself, a factor favoring economic and social progress. . . . In order for it to become a factor predominantly favorable to development, a realistic demographic policy must be formulated and applied as a well-designed, efficiently functioning part of the whole group of national development plans." Gilberto Loyo, *3 breves estudios* (México: Imprenta Arana, 1970), p. 68.

[64] Moisés Poblete Troncoso, *La explosión demográfica en América Latina* (Buenos Aires: Editorial Schapire, 1967), p. 81.

[65] María Teresa Gutiérrez de MacGregor, *Desarrollo y distribución de la población urbana en México* (México: Universidad Nacional Autónoma de México, 1965), pp. 30-31.

[66] *Novedades*, October 5, 1972.

[67] See María del Carmen Elu de Leñero, "Antecedentes y motivaciones para la planeación familiar," in María del Carmen Elu de Leñero, ed., *Mujeres que hablan: Implicaciones psico-sociales en el uso de métodos anticonceptivos* (México: Instituto Mexicano de Estudios Sociales, 1971); and María del Carmen Elu de Leñero, *¿Hacia dónde va la mujer mexicana? Proyecciones a partir de los datos de una encuesta nacional*, 2d ed. (México: Instituto Mexicano de Estudios Sociales, 1973), esp. chap. 9, "¿Es feliz la mujer casada?"

growth undercuts both the absolute rate of economic advance and its natural tendency to improve per capita living conditions.[68] Such views have been actively explored at the center, which was founded at the prestigious College of Mexico (*El Colegio de México*) in 1964, and in the pages of the center's journal, *Demografía y Economía*. In the first issue of the journal, published in 1967, Víctor Urquidi wrote that the regulation of births "every day appears to be more necessary," and subsequent articles have reiterated this theme from a variety of standpoints.[69]

Another argument, which has long been used by proponents of family planning, suggests that regulation of births is necessary in order to reduce the intolerably high number of illegal, dangerous, and immoral abortions. Ifigenia de Navarrete thus forcefully advocates contraception as a means to regulate fertility, accelerate per capita economic growth, and limit the number of illegal abortions.[70] With the official inauguration of Mexico's family-planning program in January 1973, Dr. Jorge Jiménez Cantú, the secretary of health and welfare, publicly declared that "it is better to prevent conception than to provoke abortion or to treat cases of abortion induced . . . through immoral practices."[71] In adamantly opposing abortion and the new calls for freedom regarding it,[72] some Catholic theologians outside Mexico have similarly proposed responsible contraceptive practices that strengthen the family unit and make abortion unnecessary.[73] In contrast, the Bishop of Ciudad Juárez simply issued a pastoral letter condemning

---

[68] See *Dinámica de la población de México*, esp. chap. 8, "Aspectos demográficos del crecimiento económico," pp. 227, 233-234.

[69] Víctor L. Urquidi, "El crecimiento demográfico y el desarrollo económico latinoamericano," *Demografía y Economía*, vol. 1 (1967), p. 8. Also, see Susana Lerner, "La investigación y la planeación demográficas en México," ibid.; Víctor L. Urquidi, "El desarrollo económico y el crecimiento de la población," ibid., vol. 3 (1969); Luis Olivos, "Políticas de población y desarrollo para el año 2000," ibid.; José B. Morelos, "El problema demográfico de México," ibid.; Francisco Javier Alejo and Víctor L. Urquidi, "La investigación sobre aspectos demográficos del desarrollo económico en México," ibid., vol. 4 (1970); and José B. Morelos, "El desarrollo económico y los recursos humanos en México: Un esquema conceptual," ibid., vol. 5 (1971).

[70] Navarrete, *Sobrepoblación y desarrollo económico*, pp. 31, 33-34.

[71] *Novedades*, Januady 27, 1973.

[72] See, for instance, Sharon Robins and Bruce Granger, *Having a Wonderful Abortion* (New York: Exposition Press, 1971).

[73] Bernard Häring, "A Theological Evaluation," in John T. Noonan, Jr., ed., *The Morality of Abortion: Legal and Historical Perspectives* (Cambridge: Harvard University Press, 1970), pp. 133-135. Also, see the statement by Daniel Callahan in Robert E. Hall, ed., *Abortion in a Changing World*, 2 vols. (New York: Columbia University Press, 1970), vol. 2, pp. 102-104.

abortion on any grounds, including the health of the mother.[74] Nevertheless, statistics show that the resulting problems are so extensive as to belie such rhetorical solutions. Forty percent of the married women interviewed in a Mexican national sample had undergone abortions, and 85 percent of the women understandably considered it necessary to use some form of birth control.[75]

Although such statistics on abortion undoubtedly indicate a situation where the prevention of conception seems preferable in terms of the physical and emotional health of the mother, the abortion issue as such had comparatively little impact in the 1972 reorientations of government policy. The issue can rally support behind family planning, but by itself it was certainly not strong enough to precipitate the shift in the government's position. The level of abortions has long been high. Mexico will in time liberalize her 1931 abortion laws, and numerous citizens called for such reform in 1973.[76] But while the last decade has thus involved an increase in both public and official recognition of the problem, the major change has occurred in attitudes toward abortion rather than in its general incidence.

Similarly, dissension within Catholic ranks did not prompt the alteration in the policies of the Mexican government; instead, such controversy tended to make it more feasible for that shift to take place once it was decided upon for other reasons. Family planning happens to coincide with the Church's long-run interests as an institution. Mexico's population explosion has seriously weakened and now gravely threatens the position of the Church, as the number of nominal Catholics expands far faster than the number of priests to serve them.[77] But such considerations did not alter the official posi-

---

[74] Manuel Talamás Camandari (Primer Obispo de Ciudad Juárez), *III carta pastoral sobre la inmoralidad del aborto*, April 2, 1961.

[75] Leñero Otero, *Investigación de la familia en México*, p. 156.

[76] "Abortos y planeación," *Tiempo*, vol. 63 (December 24, 1973), p. 3.

[77] See James W. Wilkie, "Statistical Indicators of the Impact of National Revolution on the Catholic Church in Mexico, 1910-1967," *Journal of Church and State*, vol. 12 (Winter 1970), pp. 96-106. In commenting on Luis Echeverría's firm campaign stand against family planning in 1969, Wilkie notes: "Though some observers felt that Echevarría's [sic] dramatic statement against population control was meant to appeal to conservative Catholics who fear such activity, others speculated that perhaps Echevarría [sic] realized that an expanding population would severly [sic] test the Church. . . . A third view claimed that Echevarría [sic] was catering to left-wing, ultra-nationalists, who maintain that Mexico must abstain from birth control in order to gain a population base which can exist politically and economically independent from the United States." Probably, the candidate of the PRI was trying to win favor from both left- and right-wing nationalists, assuming that economic growth would remain far greater than the rise in population.

tion of the Church hierarchy in Mexico before 1972, any more than they undercut traditional Mexican anticlericalism or forged an alliance of churchmen and secularists to urge the government to undertake programs of population limitation. Statements of support for the responsible parenthood program, like that of journalist Roberto Blanco Moheno, contain open warnings to the Church. As he pointedly remarked, "Priests are to serve believers in matters of the spirit and NOTHING MORE. In matters of the bed, they are totally ignorant." [78]

Are such warnings really necessary in contemporary Mexico? How much influence does the Church maintain on family matters? Some data rather misleadingly suggest that the Church has little impact in this area, but these data can easily give rise to mistaken conclusions. Just as a high level of abortion continues in Mexico despite the protestations of Church officials against it, so a curious, positive relationship exists between conscientious practice of the Catholic faith and the use of birth control techniques. Those who are most demonstrably religious in Latin America are also likely to practice birth control.[79] Leñero's national survey found the use of contraceptive techniques lowest (26.8 percent) among respondents whose religious practice was only moderate, while for the groups with either very high or no religious practice the use of contraception reached 44.9 percent and 41.8 percent, respectively. The paradox in these data is more apparent than real, since the rhythm method was the choice of a majority of the highly religious respondents who used some type of contraception. The Mexican data also confirm the general finding in Latin America that the wealthier and better-educated classes are positively inclined toward both birth control and the Church. As the income of the respondents increased, so did their use of the rhythm method and their rejection of other birth control measures. Interestingly, those with the highest levels of religious practice were also consistently those with the best knowledge of birth control.[80]

---

[78] Blanco Moheno, "Natalidad y conciencia," p. 70.

[79] See the data summarized in Tables 1 and 2 in Gustavo Pérez Ramírez, "The Catholic Church and Family Planning—Current Perspectives," in Stycos and Arias, eds., *Population Dilemma in Latin America*, p. 203.

[80] Maldonado, *Los católicos y la planeación familiar*, pp. 124, 134, 146, 148. Among the respondents with less than 1,500 pesos in monthly income who practiced family planning, 52.6 percent used rhythm, 22.6 percent the pill, and 24.8 percent other methods, while among those with monthly incomes of 10,000 pesos, 83.4 percent used rhythm, 8.8 percent the pill, and 7.8 percent other methods.

A comparison may be made between the Catholic Church and the United Nations, both transnational institutions whose official lack of positive concern for family planning before the 1970s worked to deter family-planning programs. Internationally, as population expert Phyllis Piotrow effectively demonstrates, Catholic as well as Communist opposition kept the agencies of the United Nations from aiding national family-planning programs before 1971.[81] With the declaration of 1974 as World Population Year, however, the United Nations moved toward increasingly meaningful programs, while the Church had already accepted the initiatives of the Mexican government for responsible parenthood. Claims for constructive United Nations influence suggest that the United Nations has encouraged changes in national policies by providing believable, worldwide figures on the rapid rates of demographic growth, by serving as a forum for debate on these issues, and more recently by giving increased legitimacy to those national leaders who advocate family planning.[82] During 1973, the World Health Organization responded to requests for assistance in family planning from over fifty countries.[83] While the United Nations and its functional organizations have thus taken positive initiatives, Church policies have only come to accept the initiatives of others. This is significant, however, because since 1945, the influence of the Church and Catholic doctrine in Mexico has been far greater, and more negative, than have the demographic orientations of the United Nations.

Priests, for instance, have continued significantly to shape women's attitudes. Of the respondents in the Corwin study who opposed family planning, many housewives gave religious or moral justifications for their stand, in contrast to most men, who said that the economy was growing without population control, that the country's wealth lay in its people, or that Mexico still had great resources and uncultivated lands.[84] The heavy reliance of Mexican women

[81] Phyllis Tilson Piotrow, *World Population Crisis: The United States Response* (New York: Praeger Publishers, 1973), chap. 19, "Population and Development in the United Nations." Dr. Piotrow has served as administrator of the Population Information Program at George Washington University Medical Center, as executive director of the Population Crisis Committee, and as a consultant to the United Nations on population matters.

[82] Richard Symonds and Michael Carder, *The United Nations and the Population Question, 1945-1970* (London: Chatto & Windus, 1973), p. 205.

[83] "Family Planning: A Concern for the Quality of Life," *World Health*, January 1974, pp. 3-5.

[84] Corwin, *Contemporary Mexican Attitudes*, pp. 16-19. In another sense, however, Corwin's survey suggests that Mexican women are not as committed to the Church's traditional position on family planning as was once thought. In

upon rhythm as a means of contraception [85] underlines the long-term effect of Church doctrines on cultural norms. Information from Peru suggests that regular Church attendance and being married in the Catholic Church do increase the number of children desired when the education variable is held constant.[86]

Moreover, no matter what the impact of Church teaching in this area actually is, Mexican leaders believe it to be great. When a cross-section of the elite from Mexico's governmental, religious, and private sectors was asked which groups had "great influence" on the orientations and views of Mexican families, they replied that priests had far more effect than either doctors or governmental leaders. As Table 4 reveals, some 70 percent attributed great influence to priests,

Table 4
GROUPS THAT MEXICAN LEADERS CONSIDER TO HAVE GREAT INFLUENCE UPON FAMILY ORIENTATIONS

Groups	Percent of Affirmative Responses
Priests	70
High religious authorities	69
Schoolteachers	51
Radio, cinema, and television artists	39
Newspapermen	37
Directors of religious organizations	35
Medical doctors	34
University leaders	25
Leaders of the federal government	24
Authors of books	22
Leaders of the state governments	17
Leaders of the municipal governments	16
Leaders of trade unions and peasant organizations	16
Psychologists and psychiatrists	12
Political party officials	10
Businessmen	8

Source: Luis Leñero Otero, *Investigación de la familia en México: Presentación y avance de resultados de una encuesta nacional* (México: Instituto Mexicano de Estudios Sociales, 1968), p. 177.

answering a question on whether they thought that rapid population growth was an important cause of low salaries among Mexico's laboring classes, women provided a far higher proportion of affirmative responses than did male employers or professionals.

[85] Leñero Otero, *Investigación de la familia en México*, p. 167.

[86] Stycos, *Human Fertility in Latin America*, pp. 173-174. See also chap. 10, "Social Class and Preferred Family Size in Peru," pp. 147-161.

while only 51 percent attributed it to teachers, 34 percent to doctors, and 24 percent to the national leaders of the federal government. This is in part because priests have traditionally spoken out on the subject of family life far more than have politicians, and it also reflects the high proportion of Catholic authorities included in the leadership survey,[87] but it nevertheless demonstrates the influence that Mexican leaders ascribe to the Church in family matters.

Because the role of the Church in family affairs is essentially one of legitimation, the heightening controversy over contraception among the Catholic clergy has prevented the Church from opposing new initiatives like those of the Mexican government. Not only has the Mexican Church lost much of its earlier political power and adapted to many of the nationalist goals of the revolutionary governments;[88] it has also been prey to grave divisions in the worldwide Church, which tend to weaken its strategic position still further. Despite the continuing papal prohibition of any techniques of family planning other than the rhythm method, a number of prominent Catholic spokesmen have come to advocate various ways, both in the United States [89] and in Latin America.[90] Considerable reaction against

[87] The leadership sample consisted of fifty government officials, fifty directors of Catholic lay organizations, thirty functionaries from Mexico's three leading parties, thirty members of the Church hierarchy, thirty leaders of economic organizations and trade unions, thirty doctors, and twenty newspapermen.

[88] Frederick C. Turner, "The Compatibility of Church and State in Mexico," *Journal of Inter-American Studies*, vol. 9 (October 1967).

[89] John Rock, *The Time Has Come: A Catholic Doctor's Proposals to End the Battle over Birth Control* (New York: Alfred A. Knopf, 1963); Thomas B. Mc-Donough, "Distribution of Contraceptives by the Welfare Department: A Catholic Response," in *The Problem of Population: Practical Catholic Applications* (Notre Dame: University of Notre Dame Press, 1964), pp. 94-115; John T. Noonan, Jr., *Contraception: A History of Its Treatment by the Catholic Theologians and Canonists* (Cambridge: Harvard University Press, 1965), pp. 387-533; Charles E. Curran, "Natural Law and Contemporary Moral Theology," in Curran, ed., *Contraception: Authority and Dissent* (New York: Herder and Herder, 1969), pp. 151-176; and Michael Novak, "Frequent, Even Daily Communion," in Daniel Callahan, ed., *The Catholic Case for Contraception* (London: Macmillan, 1969), pp. 92-102.

[90] See Frederick C. Turner, *Catholicism and Political Development in Latin America* (Chapel Hill: University of North Carolina Press, 1971), pp. 77-86; Dorothy Dunbar Bromley, *Catholics and Birth Control: Contemporary Views on Doctrine* (New York: Devin Adair, 1965), pp. 160-162; and Hernán Romero, *Población, desarrollo, y control de natalidad en América Latina: Prejuicios y controversias* (México: Editorial Diana, 1969), esp. pp. 149-150. For defense and analysis of the more traditional Catholic position, see *Regulación de los nacimientos* (Santiago de Chile: DESAL, 1963); Alvah W. Sulloway, *Birth Control and Catholic Doctrine* (Boston: Beacon Press, 1959); George A. Kelly, *Birth Control and Catholics* (Garden City: Doubleday & Co., 1963), esp. chap. 4, "The

the papal position on family planning met its restatement in the encyclical *Humanae vitae*.[91]

In December 1972, a collective pastoral of the Mexican bishops gave their support to the government initiatives. Opposing "what is a very real and excruciating emergency for most Mexican families: the population explosion," the message described its deleterious effects as including inadequate food, housing, and health care; unemployment; the immorality of broken homes and abortion; difficulties in education and religious training; and even "lack of self-development in the woman." The bishops praised Echeverría's program, especially its leaving of the final decision on contraception to the individual couples involved. While at one point describing the rhythm method as the only "legitimate" technique of birth control, the Mexican episcopacy, like that of Chile in 1968, said indirectly, over and over again, that couples deserve support for the private decisions that they make in this area, clearly implying that other techniques are also acceptable.[92] The public criticism that the bishops have received from more conservative Catholics[93] has not changed their orientation. Thus not only did the Church in Mexico fail to oppose the government's decision to distribute contraceptives and information forbidden in official Catholic doctrine, but the national Church leaders—sensitive to the grave dangers that the population explosion poses in Mexico—have also given their strong endorsement to the family-planning effort.

World's Answer—Contraception"; John R. Cavanagh, *The Popes, the Pill, and the People* (Milwaukee: Bruce Publishing Company, 1965); and Jean-Louis Flandrin, *L'Eglise et le Contrôle des Naissances* (Paris: Flammarion, 1970). Excellent summaries of the Catholic debate concerning contraception during the 1960s appear in Richard A. McCormick, S.J., "Notes on Moral Theology," *Theological Studies*, vol. 26 (1965), pp. 633-647; vol. 27 (1966), pp. 647-654; and vol. 28 (1967), pp. 796-800.

[91] For a solid discussion of Catholic reactions to *Humanae vitae*, see Richard A. McCormick, S.J., "Notes on Moral Theology: January-June 1969," *Theological Studies*, vol. 30 (1969), pp. 635-668.

[92] The bishops' feeling that families *should* be planned appears unequivocally in the statement that "it is for spouses to decide, in God's presence, how many children they will have in their family. Not leaving it to chance or acting out of selfish reasons, but guided by objective norms. . . ." On the specific techniques of contraception, the pastoral declares that "the decision on the means they are to take, loyally following the dictates of their conscience, ought to leave them at peace, inasmuch as they have no reason for feeling cut off from God's friendship"; that "the important thing is for man to seek, sincerely and loyally, what is the will of God for him in his particular situation"; and that, quoting Cardinal Wright, "a sound pastoral practice is always based on trust in God's mercy and Christ's pardoning power." For the full text of the pastoral, see "A Message on Responsible Parenthood," LADOC (January 1973).

[93] See, for example, Carlos Alvear Acevedo, "La paternidad responsable: Sólo la voz del Papa," *Excelsior*, March 29, 1973.

The attitudes of Mexican churchmen are not as different from those of other citizens as popular stereotypes portray them to be. When rhythm is accepted as one method of family planning, religious leaders are not much more strongly opposed to this planning than are other Mexican elites. In the Leñero Otero survey, some 39.8 percent of the religious authorities questioned favored family planning. This was less than the 49.1 percent of the physicians who did so, but the proportion of priests favoring it virtually equalled that for federal government leaders (39.4 percent), and it exceeded that for newspapermen (30.5 percent) and for businessmen (25.2 percent).[94] During the 1960s, even conservative Catholic statements stressed the need for parents to bring out "the full development of the personality" of their children[95] and to provide "responsible fatherhood and motherhood" in regard to education and economic growth.[96] With this in mind, the Echeverría administration has been prudent to explain its own policy shift in these terms.

3. Nationalism: Aid or Hindrance?

In the process of instigating the government's "responsible parenthood" program, the force of Mexican nationalism has not proved to be as rugged a barrier to innovation as many commentators had described. "Nationalist" opponents of family planning, whether they allegedly came from the far right or the extreme left, have been swallowed up in the flood of patriotic verbiage used to justify the government's new initiative. Far more than a rhetorical device or a hollow sounding board for the self-interest of politicians, nationalism in Mexico has proved to be a supple and resilient force, one that can add legitimacy even to abrupt alterations in past policies when such shifts appear to be furthering the long-range goals that the PRI leadership has set out for the nation. As political scientist Raúl Béjar Navarro has ably demonstrated, the multitude of studies dealing with the Mexican "national character" have been highly im-

---

[94] Leñero Otero, *Investigación de la familia en México*, p. 185. On the other hand, a strong group of churchmen (27.9 percent) believed that action should be taken against anti-conception campaigns, as compared to only 17.2 percent of the federal authorities who held this position.

[95] *Exhortación pastoral del Excmo. y Revmo. Sr. Dr. Dn. Fernando Romo Gutiérrez, Primer Obispo de Torreón, a los padres de familia*, March 25, 1962, p. 4.

[96] Stanislas de Lestapis, "Visión cristiana del desarrollo demográfico. Principios y orientaciones para la acción," in *La revolución demográfica: Estudio interdisciplinar del caso colombiano* (Bogotá: Centro de Investigación y Acción Social, 1966), pp. 189-196.

pressionistic,[97] and, until more survey research is conducted in Mexico, our understanding of both Mexican nationalism and the Mexican national character will remain severely limited. Some aspects of demographic change seem to promote nationalism and national awareness,[98] and the experiences of 1972 show that nationalism itself cannot block major modifications in population policies, but the linkages among these and related variables need to be more systematically explored. Even before such active exploration is undertaken, however, some recent changes in the official uses of nationalism can already be analyzed.

Like the philosopher's stone, nationalism is a tool with which political leaders in Mexico seem able to conjure on almost any subject. President Echeverría has declared that responsible parenthood includes training in patriotism as well as planning the size of the family. After watching the traditional Independence Day military parade on September 16, 1971, he told reporters that it was the duty of all mothers and fathers in Mexico to bring up their children with a profound sense of patriotism. Observing that even the youngest viewers of the Independence Day parade saluted the flag with respect and enthusiasm, he said that it was only by patriotic teaching from older family members that the goals of the *Patria* could be made meaningful to the young and could then be upheld by them in times to come.[99] The President's wife used similar words on April 29, 1972, as she likened Mexican children to soldiers who would relieve the present generation of its duties in what she called "our historical continuity." [100]

If nationalism thus remains a crucial element of political socialization in Mexico, its officially sanctioned implications for population policies have not stayed the same. Nationalist rhetoric no longer stresses the total national population as a source of power and pride. During the 1910 Revolution, Mexicans boasted of their comparatively large population, noting for instance that, although Argentina had the outstanding economy in Latin America, Mexico had more than twice as many people as the Argentine Republic.[101] A half-century later,

---

[97] Raúl Béjar Navarro, *El mito del mexicano* (México: Facultad de Ciencias Políticas y Sociales, Universidad Nacional Autónoma de México, 1968).

[98] On the influence of demographic variables on nationalism, see Frederick C. Turner, "The Implications of Demographic Change for Nationalism and Internationalism," *Journal of Politics*, vol. 27 (February 1965).

[99] Presidencia de la República, *El gobierno mexicano*, segunda epoca, no. 10 (September 1-30, 1971), pp. 327-328.

[100] Ibid., no. 17 (April 1-30, 1972), p. 118.

[101] Frederick C. Turner, *The Dynamic of Mexican Nationalism* (Chapel Hill, N.C.: University of North Carolina Press, 1968), p. 64.

despite the fact that numerous leaders in education and business expressed grave concern over the rate of population increase, nearly all of the 230 respondents who were interviewed for Corwin's study in Monterrey showed positive pride in the demographic growth of their nation and their city.[102] These orientations would seem out of place today. In June 1972, President Echeverría declared that a country was neither "great" nor "small" because of the number of its inhabitants, any more than it was because of its geographic size or its per capita wealth. Rather, he said, national greatness depended upon the hard work and the spirit of a nation's people.[103]

The linkage between nationalism and pride in population has not been one of an aggressive foreign policy in twentieth-century Mexico. As Gilberto Loyo points out, Mexico allowed its population to grow after the 1910 Revolution, not out of "exaggerated nationalism" and "obviously not with goals of aggression and [territorial] expansion," but simply because the country's leaders believed it to be underpopulated in relation to its possibilities for economic development.[104] Appeals to patriotism can also be a way to shut out internal dissent, however, and this danger has appeared in some Echeverría speeches. In his electoral campaign, he proclaimed at one point, "If in essential matters we Mexicans are united, if the dissident voices are few and isolated, if they do not achieve true popularity, we can all hoist the banner of the fatherland in order to march with great optimism toward the future."[105] Fortunately, after being elected, he established a record of dialogue with the dissident and the potentially dissident, trying to maintain the diversity that is a hallmark of the Mexican establishment.

With this objective, contemporary Mexican nationalism remains strong but not strident, a force to bring citizens together rather than to set them antagonistically apart. In a speech commemorating the centenary of Benito Juárez's death, President Echeverría thus firmly rejected foreign intervention in Mexican affairs and applauded equality of opportunity. He opposed "any form of aristocracy," but, instead of using nationalistic appeals to attack "aristocrats," spoke instead of a "constitutional and popular nationalism," of "national dignity

102 Corwin, *Contemporary Mexican Attitudes*, p. 13.

103 *Tiempo*, vol. 61 (June 12, 1972), p. 44.

104 Loyo, *Población y desarrollo económico*, pp. 158-159.

105 *Luis Echeverría: Ideario*, 6 vols. (México: Partido Revolucionario Institucional, 1970), vol. 3, p. 647. This statement was made in Tehuacán, Puebla, on January 20, 1970.

and the personal dignity of Mexicans."[106] This is still the ethos of Mexican nationalism that Arthur Whitaker characterized as "restrained and progressive."[107]

Such nationalism naturally contains significant economic components. During its first two years, the Echeverría administration assumed majority control of a number of companies, including newspapers, hotels, bus lines, mining operations, a television station, and the telephone company. There were sound reasons for this apparently "nationalistic" policy; it gave the government greater independence from the United States, as well as from foreign investors and the Mexican private sector. In 1970, the year in which Echeverría decided upon the policies that he would pursue as president, the amount of money required to service the interest and amortization of Mexico's foreign debt equalled 23.5 percent of its foreign exchange earnings, and the remittance of profits outside Mexico exceeded the amount of new foreign capital that came into the country. Two-thirds of Mexico's foreign trade and nine-tenths of its tourist income come from the United States, and former President Nixon's imposition of a temporary 10 percent import surcharge further exacerbated a situation in which Mexico's imports were rising far faster than its exports. In the context of these economic realities, it is quite natural for Echeverría to have moved to cut luxury imports through a new tax, to seek new markets for exports in Europe, Asia, and Latin America, and guardedly to restrict United States investment through the assumption of government control of selected companies and industries. That his policies have been well received in the United States demonstrates the underlying tolerance and understanding that have characterized Mexican-American relations for some time, as, in another sense, does the "low profile" of the United States with regard to checks on the population explosion in Mexico.

4. Some Implications for United States Policy

Misunderstandings and misperceptions can easily occur among statesmen and intellectuals in the United States and Latin America over the sensitive issue of population planning. As the gradualness of demographic initiatives worries some North Americans, so Latin Americans can easily interpret such concern as indication of a colonialist or racist

---

[106] *Excelsior*, July 19, 1972.

[107] Arthur P. Whitaker and David C. Jordan, *Nationalism in Contemporary Latin America* (New York: Free Press, 1966), p. 51.

mentality. Major population policies in any part of the world can be undertaken only through the governments of the nations involved, but, because the United States and other members of the world community have a genuine interest in development elsewhere, it becomes important to define what that interest really is and in what ways it can be most effectively pursued.

Mexicans who are the most sympathetic to responsible parenthood recognize the dangers posed for such policies by foreign pressure in favor of them,[108] while Latin American critics of the United States claim that its advocacy of population limitation is one sign of its imperialism. As a recent Mexican attack said, ludicrously denouncing family planning as "Nazi sterilization," the impetus for this policy comes from "the country of Watergate" and the funds of the Ford and Rockefeller foundations.[109] Tirades like that of writer José Consuegra also show profound animosity toward the North American view. After noting such "anti-Malthusian" arguments as those of Henry George and the Catholic Church, Consuegra caustically quotes *Life* magazine on the high number of schoolgirls in the United States who have had sexual intercourse. [110] In the late 1960s, the announcement of United States aid to Brazil for demographic research touched off a similar spate of anti-American denunciations in the Brazilian press. When it was reported that Protestant missionaries were clandestinely encouraging birth control, Brazilian priests and newspapermen cried out that the North Americans were trying to trick and "castrate" Brazilian women, to impede the development of Brazil, and to depopulate and perhaps internationalize the Amazon region.[111]

---

108 Luis Leñero Otero, who has directed the most comprehensive survey of Mexican attitudes toward population issues, warns that "the excuse for birth control made by the international centers of economic and political interest, which in many cases manifests itself through negative campaigns conducted by the highly developed countries for the young and poor nations, causes strong reactions that interfere with the problems of family planning." Leñero Otero, "The Mexican Urbanization Process and Its Implications," p. 873.

109 F. Carmona Nenclares, "Esterilización: Moderno bálsamo de fierabrás," *Excelsior*, August 24, 1973.

110 José Consuegra, *El control de la natalidad como el imperialismo* (Buenos Aires: Editorial Galerna, 1969), p. 111. For very different interpretations of Malthus's message and its contemporary relevance, see "Malthus in Retrospect," *Population Bulletin*, vol. 22 (February 1966); and S. Chandrasekhar, "Malthus: Father of Demography," *Population Review*, vol. 13 (January-December 1969). Malthus did not, of course, advocate contraception in the modern sense.

111 Francisco Lagge Pessoa, ed., *Brasil. Control de la natalidad, agosto, 1966-1967: Algunos documentos clave* (Cuernavaca: CIDOC, 1967), esp. pp. 4/70-4/80, 4/110-4/113, and 4/125-4/128. This uproar has subsided, and Brazilian nationalism has flourished with the new movement to open the Amazon basin, but only a few

Such opponents of family planning frequently make North American statements appear to reflect a self-interested *gringo* plot, as when professors at the Catholic University of Chile quote Kingsley Davis as saying: "The formidable inflation of population in the less developed nations is not in our national interest."[112]

This raises the question of what the United States national interest really is. Statesmen and scholars in the United States are indeed worried about the precipitate growth of population in many developing countries, largely out of concern for the United States national interest rather than because of innate humanitarianism or paternalistic kindness. From the standpoint of actual North American interests, however, the motivations are not those that foreign critics usually mention;[113] they do not stem from fear that growing populations overseas will create such strong economies as to overthrow United States neocolonialism, or will promote the less-developed countries' military power to oppose the United States, or will increase the preponderance of colored over Caucasian peoples. Although an earlier generation did tend to associate rapid demographic growth and a massive national population with these elements of political power and prestige,[114] the level of thinking on these problems has become more sophisticated in the last decade. Among nations with more than 40 or 50 million people, it is recognized that the *quality* of a national population counts for far more—in terms of power as well as more aesthetic values—than does either its size or its rate of population growth.

---

years ago these xenophobic fears were vociferous. On the gradual evolution of demographic planning in Brazil, see Thomas G. Sanders, *The Politics of Population in Brazil*, American Universities Field Staff Reports, East Coast South America Series, vol. 15 (April 1971).

[112] Armand and Michèle Mattelart, *La Problématique du Peuplement Latino-Américain* (Paris: Editions Universitaires, 1964), p. 189.

[113] See J. Mayone Stycos, "Opinions of Latin-American Intellectuals on Population Problems and Birth Control," *The Annals*, no. 360 (July 1965); and J. Mayone Stycos, "Opposition to Family Planning in Latin America: Conservative Nationalism," *Demography*, vol. 5 (1968).

[114] See Katherine Organski and A. F. K. Organski, *Population and World Power* (New York: Alfred A. Knopf, 1961), esp. chap. 2, "Population and Power," and chap. 7, "National Population Policies." For a current example of this demographic determinism, which concludes with the unlikely assumption that "the prospects for fifty years hence are of a world in which both the United States and Soviet Russia have fallen out of the race, a world dominated by the Asian countries, with India and China in the lead," see Colin Clark, "World Power and Population," in Walt Anderson, ed., *Politics and Environment: A Reader in Ecological Crisis* (Pacific Palisades, Calif.: Goodyear, 1970).

In terms of ultimate confrontations, as opposed to conventional or guerrilla wars, for example, military power derives not from a large standing army but from technological breakthroughs in very complex armament systems. These breakthroughs are more likely in countries with high educational levels and with the heavy investments in research that are impeded when a nation must cope with the expenses of feeding more and more people. Similarly, if United States strategists actually wished to maintain "neocolonialist" control over their trading partners, they rationally would encourage the ballooning of foreign populations to keep down per capita income abroad, expand the markets for United States exports, and prevent the heavy investments in university education and research that are necessary to allow the developing countries to overcome the technological lead of the United States. It is more difficult to disprove the psychological argument on North American fears of high fertility among colored foreign peoples, but it is illogical on at least three grounds: (1) the colored peoples of the world already vastly outnumber Caucasians and will continue to do so even if the fertility levels of the two groups come into line, (2) Caucasians in Europe and North America have already greatly reduced their own levels of fertility, and (3) more enlightened and tolerant attitudes toward racial differences and miscegenation are gradually arising in the United States.

If these old bugaboos of militarism, racism, and colonialism are not behind the evolving United States concern about the population explosion, then what is the United States national interest in regard to family planning abroad? Increasingly, despite some contrary opinions,[115] it is expressed in terms of ecological constraints and the growing disparity of per capita income between "rich" and "poor"

---

[115] Barry Commoner suggests that, since the ecological crisis in the industrialized nations has come about more from the use of new technologies and synthetic products than it has from population increase, the developed countries ought to return to greater dependence on the natural products of the Third World rather than on synthetics. This interpretation is open to question, however. Even if technological innovation and industrialization are major causes of ecological problems, population increase is also a serious contributing factor, since—at the standard of living to which the citizens of both the more and the less developed nations aspire—each person comes to consume a high level of natural and/or synthetically produced resources. The fewer consumers there are at any given resource level, the more there will be for them to consume and the lower will be the potential drain on resources. Extensive excerpts from Dr. Commoner's address before a meeting of the American College of Obstetricians and Gynecologists are cited in "Fertility Control Won't Solve Ecology Crisis," Modern Medicine, September 20, 1971.

nations.[116] Even with the "green revolution" and other advances in agricultural and industrial technology, the exhaustible resources of the world are being used up at a faster and faster pace. This naturally alarms thoughtful citizens in the United States, where high standards of living consume an exorbitant share of the world's resources. Fears are exacerbated by the spectres of industrialization and nationalism abroad, where citizens of the less-developed countries come to consume more resources among themselves after their economies have gained the capacity to let them do so, and where their national interest leads them to seize control of their own resources, much as Mexico did with oil holdings in 1938. Even with growing affluence at home and evident desires in some quarters to isolate the United States from entanglements and commitments overseas, the country cannot move far toward autarky, especially given its need for raw materials and for goods produced by lower paid foreign labor. United States leaders also recognize that per capita living standards are advancing far more swiftly in the developed than in the less-developed countries, steadily widening the gap between them. Since the developed countries have far lesser rates of population increase than do those with lower levels of per capita income, the United States takes more than a humanitarian interest in family planning and greater economic advances for the Third World.

If the national interest of the United States is defined in this way, then what policies should be pursued? First, ecological considerations and the force of example suggest that the United States must continue to improve family-planning facilities at home. This cuts down on births where per capita resource use is especially high, and in the long run it is likely to be the most convincing manifestation of concern for overpopulation around the world. Latin Americans respond favorably to such examples, as in a recent article in the *Revista Mexicana de Sociología*, which reported the millions of dollars that the United States government came to spend each year in the 1970s to provide family-planning education and services, and which went on to suggest that Latin American countries also should combine population policies with their programs of economic development.[117]

---

[116] See Paul R. Ehrlich and Anne H. Ehrlich, *Population, Resources, Environment: Issues in Human Ecology* (San Francisco: W. H. Freeman, 1970); Jean Mayer, "Toward a Non-Malthusian Population Policy," *Milbank Memorial Fund Quarterly*, vol. 47 (July 1969); "Man's Population Predicament," *Population Bulletin*, vol. 27 (April 1971); and Dennis C. Pirages and Paul R. Ehrlich, *Ark II: Social Response to Environmental Imperatives* (New York: Viking Press, 1974).

[117] Rubens Vaz da Costa, "Crescimento populacional e desenvolvimento econômico," *Revista Mexicana de Sociología*, vol. 34 (April-June 1972), p. 324.

Second, the United States can aid other nations as well as itself through financing medical research in contraceptive techniques and sociological research on the causes and consequences of population increase.[118] Public and private grants from the United States are a limited source of such support, however, and if other governments are serious in trying to deal with their own population problems, they must increasingly subsidize the costs of research. Third, the United States can assist family-planning programs if it is asked to do so by international organizations or, in some cases, by a foreign government. Such aid should be extended under international auspices whenever possible, and all those involved with it must remember that family planning can at best be only one component of national development plans to improve living standards.

As these types of United States assistance have multiplied, noninterference in the internal political decisions of other countries has become more and more essential. Quakers from the United States have unobtrusively worked in Mexico to change attitudes toward the population explosion since the 1940s, and in the 1960s a significant amount of aid came from the Ford Foundation and the International Planned Parenthood Federation.[119] The United States dollar commitment to assisting foreign countries in population matters has grown considerably, from the initial half-million dollars in research funds that the United States Public Health Service contributed to the World Health Organization in 1965, to the 96 million dollars provided for family-planning activities abroad in 1971.[120]

Government spokesmen have recognized that the crucial decisions on the use of contraceptives ultimately have to be made by individuals around the world, who are either encouraged or discouraged in their efforts by the action or inaction of their own political leaders. The vital role of national governments has been appreciated even by those whose strategy has been to avoid confrontations with Latin American regimes, such as Dr. Edgar Berman, the former

---

[118] A persuasive argument to this effect is Valerie K. Oppenheimer, "Population," *Headline Series*, no. 206 (June 1971), pp. 85-86.

[119] For summaries of the highly significant research projects that the Ford Foundation has supported in Mexico, see *Ford Foundation in Mexico and Central America* (n.p., 1969), pp. 4-11; and Oscar Harkavy, Lyle Saunders, and Anna L. Southam, "An Overview of the Ford Foundation's Strategy for Population Work," *Demography*, vol. 5 (1968), p. 551.

[120] A good summary of the activities of the United States government, both domestic and foreign, is Lynn C. Landman, "USA Government and Family Planning," *IPPF Medical Bulletin*, vol. 6 (August 1972). Also, see R. T. Ravenhold, "The A.I.D. Population and Family Planning Program—Goals, Scope, and Progress," *Demography*, vol. 5 (1968).

Agency for International Development consultant whose discussions with Latin American leaders and initiatives toward private and international organizations stimulated positive concern with population problems under the Alliance for Progress after 1962.[121] As Berman has said, governments must ultimately act because "they alone have the organization and resources to deal effectively on the scale required," and "national action can only follow national policy."[122] Reiterating this realistic approach from the Mexican point of view, Antonio Carrillo Flores has recently declared that "No country will define its [population] policy with world problems as its number one priority. We live in a world where each country considers in the first instance its own national interests."[123]

With good reason, therefore, United States dollars have not been so lavishly expended as to undermine seriously national attempts at reforming population policies in Mexico and the other Latin American republics. Early in his first term, former President Nixon stressed that the United Nations should assume leadership in responding to world population pressures, and that, in addition to assisting United Nations programs, the United States should provide bilateral support in family planning only if other nations request it and only if "the services we help to make available can be freely accepted or rejected by the individuals who receive them."[124] With this still the basic American policy, Secretary of State Henry Kissinger declared in a United Nations speech in 1974 that joint action—including "significant assistance" from such developed countries as the United States—is needed to reduce the dangerous worldwide imbalance between food and population growth, which threatens not only the material progress of nations but also the stability of the world.[125] Reemphasizing his strategy on September 18, 1974, President Ford said at the United Nations that the United States would make its food resources

---

[121] On Berman's activities, see Piotrow, *World Population Crisis*, pp. 84-87.

[122] Edgar F. Berman, "Population and Foreign Policy," in *The Problem of Population: Educational Considerations*, pp. 187, 195. For a cogent, frequently bitter analysis of the contradictions and limitations in United States policy on family planning through the middle 1960s see J. Mayone Stycos, "Family Planning and American Goals," in Chaplin, ed., *Population Policies and Growth in Latin America*.

[123] Quoted in "Se desea orientar, no imponer el control natal: Carrillo Flores," *Novedades*, January 11, 1973.

[124] Richard Nixon, press release from the White House, July 18, 1969, p. 2.

[125] From a speech on "Challenges of Interdependence" by Henry A. Kissinger at the Sixth Special Session of the United Nations General Assembly, New York City, April 15, 1974 (news release from the Bureau of Public Affairs, Department of State), p. 5.

even more available to meet world needs in exchange for cooperation on the provision of petroleum in a "global strategy for food and energy."[126]

United States leaders thus show a willingness to share increasingly scarce food supplies, even at the short-term political cost of raising domestic food prices in an inflationary economy, and at the long-term ecological cost of taking substantial acreage out of the "soil bank" and using the land to ameliorate world hunger now rather than letting it lie fallow for greater production in the future. It is no wonder that, in the context of these costs, President Ford and others should be concerned about the continuing 2 percent annual rise in world population, which threatens to double world population once again in the next thirty-five years, or that he should attempt to link United States food policies to the energy crisis, which has hit many less-developed countries very hard in their reduced abilities to import petroleum and to maintain high crop yields with petroleum-based fertilizers. But when Yankees protest their specific concern for the population explosion and related issues in Latin America and other parts of the Third World, they are more often offering deeply felt expressions of sympathy than they are, as Consuegra and others argue, providing a smoke screen behind which to hide selfish attempts to control the resources and the economies of less powerful nations. Even so, because of the danger of provoking negative reactions, such statements should continue in most instances to be pronounced only quietly by unofficial spokesmen.

Conclusions

The new initiatives of the Mexican government toward "responsible parenthood" confirm certain assumptions about both the Mexican political system and the chances for innovations in demographic policies in Latin America. Faced by emotional opposition from Catholic nationalists on the far right and Marxist intellectuals on the far left, the Echeverría administration has nevertheless steered a pragmatic, generally centrist course, responding to the real needs of the Mexican people. Through this type of responsiveness, the Mexican system provides underlying stability, the basis for renewed economic growth, and an active commitment to distribute more widely the benefits of greater national prosperity. Mexico has fallen victim

---

[126] David Anable, "U.S. Food Offer Tied to Cooperation on Oil—Ford Warns U.N. of Need for Global Strategy," *Christian Science Monitor*, September 19, 1974.

41

neither to the crisis of accommodation within the PRI, about which Raymond Vernon warned,[127] nor to a continuing inactivity in family planning. Echeverría has taken decisive action on the population front as well as in other areas, thus revealing once again the viability of Mexico's political institutions through their ability to adapt to new circumstances and newly appreciated challenges.

The emerging policies and the rallying of support for them also demonstrate the essential flexibility and constructiveness of Mexican nationalism. This nationalism does not lead to aggression against neighboring states, as it did in Nazi Germany, and it does not divide Mexicans into antagonistic groups, as it tended to do in Peronist Argentina.[128] Instead, as utilized by the governing elite, Mexican nationalism wins support for policies—and policy innovations—that are designed to implement the popular goals of the Mexican Revolution. In part, the fact that appeals for a nationalist consensus behind "responsible parenthood" have not proved to be more divisive indicates once again the strength of the PRI, the Mexican political elite, and its effectiveness in symbolic manipulation. The absence of profound opposition to the new policies also demonstrates a widespread desire for family-planning information and the genuine force of the population explosion that tends to make even adamant nationalists reconsider its effects. From the standpoint of United States foreign policy, the reorientation confirms the appropriateness of a lack of pressure or interference. It is certainly best that the Mexican government has acted in its own way, in its own time, to deal with its own country's problems.

Mexico has come to lead other nations in its public concern for population growth. Antonio Carrillo Flores, one of Mexico's most distinguished statesmen, served as the secretary general of the United Nations World Population Conference in 1974, and although the conference finally took place in Bucharest, Rumania, Mexico in 1972 had offered to be the host country.[129] Carrillo Flores played a highly constructive, mediating role at the conference, where considerable

---

[127] Raymond Vernon, *The Dilemma of Mexico's Development: The Roles of the Private and Public Sectors* (Cambridge: Harvard University Press, 1963), esp. chap. 7, "The Mexican Dilemma."

[128] K. H. Silvert, "The Costs of Anti-Nationalism: Argentina," in Silvert, ed., *Expectant Peoples: Nationalism and Development* (New York: Random House, 1963).

[129] "Carrillo Flores va a Nueva York. Pedirá México la sede de la Conferencia Mundial de Población," *Novedades*, October 25, 1972. For the secretary general's view of the meeting, see Carrillo Flores, "The Significance of the World Population Conference."

conflict appeared between spokesmen for the more developed countries, who claimed that population limitation was necessary to reduce poverty and hunger and to conserve the environment and dwindling supplies of raw materials, and the representatives of the less-developed countries, who criticized the high rates of per capita resource use in the more affluent nations, who saw demographic change as only one dimension of their own economic development, and who advocated sharing the world's wealth in a more egalitarian fashion, as through grants or higher prices for their export commodities. In a context where Nicolae Ceausescu, the president of Rumania, blamed "neo-colonialist exploitation" for the income gap between richer and poorer nations, and where he exclaimed that Rumania would go right on trying to raise its population to 25 million by 1980, Carrillo Flores demonstrated tact and realism in telling the conference that, although many delegates had agreed that the rate of population growth must be slowed, "it is also understandable that several nations in Europe, Africa and Latin America, where the objectives and situations are different, look at the problem in a different way." [130]

Before Mexican leaders took their initiatives, both at home and in the international community, no Latin American government had established quantitative goals for changes that it hoped to see in its pattern of demographic growth,[131] and Colombia and Chile were the only large nations in the region to have made population policies a formal part of their development plans. With the alterations in demographic policy set out in 1972, Mexico is thus once again becoming an innovator in the Latin American sphere, as she traditionally has been in such fields as agrarian reform. Recently, the director of the United Nations Fund for Population Activities cited Mexico as one of the most progressive Latin American nations in this regard.[132] It remains to be seen just how vigorous the government's actions will continue to be, and how much effect they will have upon the growth of population, but at least the president has placed the considerable prestige of his government behind a major reorientation of priorities. If most citizens can be made to appreciate the importance of family planning, it will help significantly in the continuing realization of the goals of Mexico's Revolution.

---

[130] *Facts on File*, vol. 34 (August 24, 1974), pp. 679-680.

[131] See "Population Trends and Policy Alternatives in Latin America," *Economic Bulletin for Latin America*, vol. 16 (1971).

[132] Rafael Salas said that "in Latin America, there is a breakthrough with Chile's first nationwide program and another planned by Mexico." Quoted in the *New York Times*, July 16, 1972.

Cover and book design: Pat Taylor